D1257907

1ST
IN FASHION
x x x x x

MARY QUANT
MINISKIRT MAKER

REBECCA FELIX

**Checkerboard
Library**

An Imprint of Abdo Publishing
abdopublishing.com

ABDOPUBLISHING.COM

Published by Abdo Publishing, a division of ABDO, PO Box 398166, Minneapolis, Minnesota 55439.
Copyright © 2018 by Abdo Consulting Group, Inc. International copyrights reserved in all countries.
No part of this book may be reproduced in any form without written permission from the publisher.
Checkerboard Library™ is a trademark and logo of Abdo Publishing.

Printed in the United States of America, North Mankato, Minnesota
062017
092017

Design: Emily O'Malley, Mighty Media, Inc.
Production: Emily O'Malley, Mighty Media, Inc.
Series Editor: Katherine Hengel Frankowski
Cover Photographs: AP Images (left); Shutterstock (right)
Interior Photographs: Alamy, pp. 9, 11, 13, 14, 17, 27; AP Images, pp. 19, 23; iStockphoto, pp. 20 (middle), 21 (top); Shutterstock, pp. 5, 20 (bottom), 21 (middle), 21 (bottom), 25; Wikimedia Commons, pp. 7, 20 (top)

Publisher's Cataloging-in-Publication Data

Names: Felix, Rebecca, author.
Title: Mary Quant: miniskirt maker / by Rebecca Felix.
Other titles: Miniskirt maker
Description: Minneapolis, MN : Abdo Publishing, 2018. | Series: First in fashion |
    Includes bibliographical references and index.
Identifiers: LCCN 2016962503 | ISBN 9781532110757 (lib. bdg.) |
    ISBN 9781680788600 (ebook)
Subjects: LCSH: Quant, Mary, 1934 - --Juvenile literature. | Fashion designer--
    Great Britain--Biography--Juvenile literature. | Women fashion designers--
    Great Britain--Biography--Juvenile literature.
Classification: DDC 746.92092 [B]--dc23
LC record available at http://lccn.loc.gov/2016962503

CONTENTS

x x x ~~~ x x x

SHORT SUCCESS

It's Saturday, and you are shopping at the mall. You see some skirts in a storefront display. Some of the skirts are **denim** with pockets and zippers. Others have bright patterns and colors. Each of the skirts is youthful, fun, and short. You've found the miniskirts!

Miniskirts have **hemlines** located a few inches above the knee. Some rise even higher than that! Short skirts have been around since ancient times. But in the 1960s, designer Mary Quant helped them become a major fashion trend. In doing so, she became one of the first designers to make clothing aimed at young people.

Quant's miniskirts helped create a fashion revolution. Young women wore miniskirts to **rebel**, show independence, and be fashionable. The supershort hemlines on miniskirts made headlines. They became popular worldwide. Quant's miniskirts shocked some and thrilled others. Ever since, they've been fashion icons.

Miniskirts of varying lengths, designs, and colors are worn by people around the world.

A SHORT HISTORY

Miniskirts may have surprised some people in the 1960s. But they've been around for a long time. In fact, an ancient Egyptian figurine shows a female in a short skirt. This figurine is thought to be from 5400 BCE!

Still, throughout history, most women wore ankle- or floor-length skirts. However, in the 1920s, some American women began wearing calf-length dresses and skirts. These women were known as **flappers**. At the time, many people considered calf-length garments **rebellious**. But flappers liked how shorter garments made dancing easier.

In the 1940s and 1950s, some US and European models wore very short skirts. Film and TV actors did too. Some people thought these short garments were improper. But most accepted entertainers in short skirts onscreen.

By the 1960s, many young women began regularly wearing miniskirts. These women became a symbol of

Flappers rebelled against society by cutting their hair short and wearing minimalist clothing.

female **empowerment**, youth, and independence. A young English designer named Mary Quant was one of the fashion trendsetters driving this change.

ART EDUCATION

Mary Quant was born on February 11, 1934, in London, England. Her parents, Jack and Mary, were teachers. Both came from Wales, in southwest Great Britain.

Education was important to the Quant family. Young Mary graduated from Blackheath High School and attended Goldsmiths College of Art in London. There, she graduated with a degree in art education.

After college, Mary became an **apprentice** to a Danish hat maker. At first, she helped design hats. Later, she created dresses and other items of clothing. At that time, most clothing designs were aimed at adults. Clothing for children and teens mirrored adult styles.

But many young people wanted to dress

FASHION FACTOID

As a young girl, Quant used to raise the **hemline** of her school uniform. She thought this made the outfit "more exciting looking."

Quant's passion for fashion and design lasted her entire life.

differently than adults. Some even adapted their own garments to make them **unique**. Mary recognized young men and women's desire for youthful fashions. She wanted to create clothing that reflected young people's spirit and style. So, Mary decided to open her own shop.

BAZAAR BOUTIQUE

In 1955, Quant and two partners opened Bazaar, a **boutique** clothing store in London. One partner was Quant's Goldsmiths classmate Alexander Plunkett-Greene. He was the boutique's fashion executive. The other partner was her friend Archie McNair. He handled the store's business dealings. Quant was Bazaar's buyer and designer.

Bazaar sold clothing that was designed by art students Quant knew. It also sold clothing that Quant designed. Quant's design ideas often came to her quickly. She could create a piece of clothing in just one night. Then she'd sell it in the store the next day! Quant's designs usually featured bright colors and bold designs. Her garments' shapes were often **geometric** and **symmetrical**.

The artful clothing sold at Bazaar reflected the **culture** outside the shop. Bazaar was on King's Road, a major street in a south London neighborhood called Chelsea.

Quant with her business partner Alexander Plunkett-Greene, whom she later married

The area was popular with young, creative people. Many artists, designers, models, and musicians spent time there. Bazaar's artistic displays and **chic**, fresh feel reflected the youthful Chelsea **culture**.

FASHION REVOLUTION

Quant's shop on King's Road was immediately successful. In 1957, Quant married her business partner Plunkett-Greene. That same year, Quant opened Bazaar's second location in Knightsbridge, a shopping district in West London. Both Bazaar stores **thrived** throughout the 1950s and 1960s.

The Bazaar stores were successful because they appealed emotionally to England's youth. In 1945, **World War II** ended. England was one of many countries that fought in the war. After the war, many young English people rejected traditions. They **rebelled** against anything old-fashioned, including clothing. They found the fresh styles they were looking for at Bazaar.

Bazaar's success was also powered by England's post-war economy. During the 1950s and 1960s, English citizens were no longer focused on the war. After years of **rationing**, people felt ready to freely spend their money.

With an improved economy, young people in England could afford to spend money on clothing that reflected their personal styles.

During that same time, England's government was creating new jobs. Many of these new jobs were filled by young people. These young adults wanted to buy trendy clothing that reflected their youth and success. The clothes Quant sold at Bazaar matched their desires.

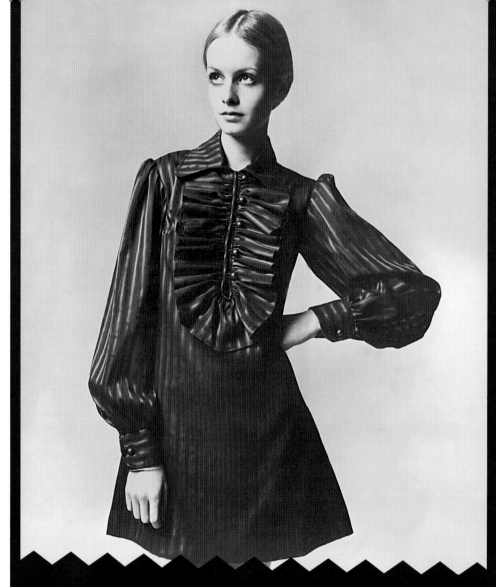

Famous model Twiggy wore many of Quant's designs in the 1960s, including miniskirts. Young people were inspired by Twiggy's style and bought their own miniskirts.

QUANT'S INFLUENCES

Quant created fashion inspired by youth. Her designs were often influenced by childhood experiences. For example, she drew inspiration from the outfits young girls wore to dance class. These included pleated skirts and leather flats that looked like ballerina shoes.

Quant was also influenced by **beatniks**. Most beatnik fashion was **minimalist**. Shapes were basic. Garments didn't have a lot of frills, buttons, or other details. Beatnik styles were usually very tight-fitting. They typically came in black or other dark colors.

In the 1960s, Quant began designing beatnik-style clothing. But her designs were a bit more colorful. They became known as part of the "mod" style. Like beatnik styles, mod clothing was tight and minimal. But mod styles used bright colors and color-blocked patterns.

Shift dresses and **pencil skirts** were popular mod styles for women in the 1960s. These items sold very well at both Bazaar shops. But many young women asked for one key adjustment. They wanted the **hemlines** to be higher up on the leg!

SUPPLY & DEMAND

In the 1960s, many young women in London were asking clothing shop owners for shorter skirts. So, Quant and many other London-based designers gave these women what they wanted. Soon, short skirts and dresses were being sold throughout London.

Quant shortened her **shift dresses** high above the knee. Her skirts got shorter too, exposing more of women's legs. Quant called these new, smaller garments miniskirts. The name stuck!

Today, historians disagree on who invented the first miniskirt. But Quant herself credits those London-based

MINI NAME

Quant named miniskirts after the Mini Cooper, her favorite car. She felt the car had similar qualities to the skirt. Quant said that both were "**exuberant**, young, flirty."

Quant often wore miniskirts herself while working with customers.

shoppers. She says they were the real inventors of the style!

The original inventor of the miniskirt may remain unknown. But most historians agree that Quant was responsible for making miniskirts a major trend. She also kept the trend alive during a worldwide **scandal**.

SCANDALOUS SKIRTS

Miniskirts soon became popular outside London. By the early 1960s, young women across England were wearing them. At that time, many designers were making miniskirts. But Quant's skirts were the best-known.

The popularity of Quant's miniskirts had a lot to do with Bazaar. The **boutique** had become known as a place where young people who cared about fashion shopped. Quant's miniskirt was also the most famous because she had given the short garment its catchy name.

In 1962, US clothing store JC Penney began selling Quant's miniskirts. Some US leaders spoke out against the short garments. They felt Quant's short skirts were **scandalous** because they showed too much of women's legs. Other world leaders agreed. During the 1960s, miniskirts were even banned in some countries!

But Quant embraced the criticism. In fact, she felt that **controversy** was a part of the miniskirt's purpose! Quant said "a miniskirt was a way of **rebelling**." Her minis were meant to fall about four inches (10 cm) below the wearer's buttocks. Though others disapproved of this length, Quant continued to champion the trend.

Young women across London protested in favor of the miniskirt.

FASHION
TIME MACHINE

CRINOLINE SKIRT, 1850s The crinoline skirt was a large, bell-shaped skirt. The skirt got its shape from stiff wire bent in a hoop shape. A dress was then attached and worn over the metal hoop.

POODLE SKIRT, 1950s Girls often wore poodle skirts in the 1950s. The knee-length skirt was made from felt and featured a patch design, usually of a poodle.

MINISKIRT, 1960s Young women **rebelled** against society by shortening the **hemlines** of their skirts in the 1960s. The miniskirt is still one of the most popular skirt styles!

MAXI SKIRT, 1970s Maxi skirts of the 1970s were loose-fitting, flowy, and ankle-length. They were often made of lightweight fabrics. Some were solid colors while others were patterned. Maxi skirts come back into fashion often, most recently in the 2010s!

RAH-RAH SKIRT, 1980s The name *rah-rah* comes from cheerleading. These short, pleated skirts are often worn by cheerleaders and other athletes. Their short length allows wearers freedom of movement. Today they are worn for fashion as well as sports.

DENIM MINISKIRT, 2000s In the 2000s, **denim** miniskirts became very popular. These have a similar style to denim jeans, with a zipper, a button, belt loops, and back pockets. And, like jeans, denim skirts come in many different shades and styles.

BOOKS, BUSINESS & TITLES

〰〰〰

The 1960s was a very successful decade for Quant. Her shops were **thriving**, and she was well-known for her miniskirts. She also had a successful **cosmetics** line, which she sold in her stores. Quant's cosmetics, like her clothing, were youthful, fun, and fresh. They were as popular with young women in England as the miniskirt.

In 1966, Quant was honored for her influence on the fashion world. Queen Elizabeth II named her an Officer of the Order of the British Empire (OBE). This title is given to people who have become nationally famous in their fields. That same year, Quant published her **autobiography**, *Quant by Quant*. It was the first of five books she would publish.

In 1969, Quant was **inducted** into the British Fashion Council Hall of Fame. In 1970, Quant and Plunkett-Greene

Quant accepted her OBE at Buckingham Palace in London.

had a son, Orlando. Quant continued to design clothing and **cosmetics** throughout the 1970s and 1980s. She began designing household goods in the 1970s as well.

MUSEUMS AND MORE HONORS

In 1973, the London Museum opened a 1960s fashion exhibit. Quant helped produce some of the displays that highlighted how she had influenced London fashion. She continued her museum work. From 1976 to 1978, she was an advisor for the Victoria and Albert Museum in London.

Quant had closed her Bazaar locations in 1971. But she ran her **cosmetics** company until 2000. Meanwhile, she wrote several books about cosmetics and fashion. Quant wrote books through the 2010s.

Quant continued to earn honors for her work in fashion. In 2015, she was named a Dame Commander of the OBE. This title is given to women whose work is inspirational or important. Dame Commander Quant and

COLORFUL CAR DESIGN

In 1988, Quant designed a special edition of the Mini Cooper called a Mini Designer. She chose to cover its seats in black-and-white stripes. The trim on the seats was bright red. The seatbelts were also red. The exteriors of Quant's Minis came in two colors. They were either diamond white or jet black.

Plunkett-Green lived together in England until his death in 1990. Quant remained there. In 2016, she celebrated her eighty-second birthday.

SMALL SKIRT, BIG IMPACT

The miniskirt was one of the most popular fashion trends of the 1960s. But miniskirts were more than just popular. They launched a whole new fashion class! Before miniskirts, clothing designed specifically for young adults didn't exist. But once miniskirts went **mainstream**, a vibrant, new fashion style was born.

Quant was at the front of this new style. She was among the first designers to create garments for young adults. Quant started out wanting to give young people their own style. In the end, she helped launch a style revolution. Her miniskirt became a sign of independence and **rebellion** worldwide.

Today, miniskirts come in many materials and shapes. Some are designed for school uniforms. Others are for playing tennis. Some people still feel miniskirts are too short. But these garments aren't going anywhere. They remain a symbol of modern fashion and youth.

Quant continued to influence fashion in her later life by attending fashion shows.

TIMELINE

xxx xxx

1934

Mary Quant is born on February 11, in London, England.

1955

Quant and her partners open Bazaar, a clothing boutique in London.

1957

Quant opens a second Bazaar location in London. She marries Alexander Plunkett-Greene.

1960s

Quant begins designing very short skirts at her customers' requests. She names them miniskirts.

1966

Quant is named an Officer of the Order of the British Empire (OBE).

1969

Quant is inducted into the British Fashion Council Hall of Fame.

1970

Quant's son, Orlando, is born.

1973

The London Museum opens an exhibit on 1960s fashion featuring Quant.

2015

Quant is named a Dame Commander of the OBE.

GLOSSARY

xxx ⋀⋀⋀

apprentice—a person who learns a trade or a craft from a skilled worker.

autobiography—a story of a person's life that is written by himself or herself.

beatnik—a member of an unofficial group of young Americans that formed in the 1950s and 1960s who rejected traditions and expressed themselves through unique art, music, and fashion.

boutique—a small, fashionable store.

chic (SHEEK)—fashionable or stylish.

controversy—a discussion marked by strongly different views.

cosmetics—products used to make hair or skin more attractive.

culture—the customs, arts, and tools of a nation or a people at a certain time.

denim—a type of cotton fabric woven with a pattern of diagonal ribs and lines.

empowerment—a social process that helps people gain control over their own lives.

exuberant—very enthusiastic or cheerful.

flapper—a young woman from 1910s and 1920s who rebelled against rules and conventions.

geometric—made up of straight lines, circles, and other simple shapes.

hemline—the bottom edge of a dress, skirt, coat, or pants legs.

induct—to admit as a member.

mainstream—the ideas, attitudes, activities or trends that are regarded as normal or dominant in society.

minimalist—relating to or being as small or revealing as possible.

pencil skirt—a straight, narrow skirt.

ration—to control the amount of something people can have.

rebel—to resist or disobey authority. Someone who rebels is rebellious. The act of rebelling is called a rebellion.

scandal—an action that shocks people and disgraces those connected with it. Something that does this is scandalous.

shift dress—a short, sleeveless dress that hangs from the shoulders and has been popular since the 1960s.

symmetrical—having two halves that are the same.

thrive—to do well.

unique (yoo-NEEK)—being the only one of its kind.

World War II—from 1939 to 1945, fought in Europe, Asia, and Africa. Great Britain, France, the United States, the Soviet Union, and their allies were on one side. Germany, Italy, Japan, and their allies were on the other side.

WEBSITES

To learn more about First in Fashion, visit **abdobooklinks.com**. These links are routinely monitored and updated to provide the most current information available.

INDEX